Divided We Stand: Reason Over Religion, Region and Politics

SMITH KHABRI

CONTENTS

FORWARD

One question has always haunted me: Why, on a planet we all share, do we divide ourselves over Gods, borders, and power? This book is my attempt to understand that question and to challenge it. Every day, I witness the grip of division. Neighbours clash over faith. Nations fight over invisible lines on a map. Leaders fuel fear just to win votes. We are one species, breathing the same air. Yet we build walls. Religious walls. Regional walls. Political walls. And these walls tear us apart.

This struggle is not confined to history books or breaking news. It shows up in our hesitation to help when floods strike, when viruses spread, and when technology races ahead of our values. Time and again, I have asked myself: Why do we choose conflict when our survival depends on unity?

This book is not just an analysis. It is a challenge. I have spent countless hours exploring Wikipedia, Britannica, history books, and YouTube documentaries to piece together a broader picture of human conflict. From crusades to genocides, from revolutions to riots, I have traced how our divisions, shaped by instinct, belief, geography, and ambition, have cost us lives, heritage, and hope.

Yet history offers another truth. We are capable of choosing a different path. Nations have signed treaties. Science has brought strangers together for a common cause. Communities have healed through truth and reconciliation. It is reason that lights the way forward, not rivalry. We are not destined to remain divided. We can choose unity if we have the courage to think clearly and compassionately.

This book is for everyone. It does not matter who you are, where you live, what you believe, or what language you speak. It speaks to every religion, every caste, every political view. The questions it raises and the answers it seeks are relevant to every human being alive today.

So I invite you to reflect. Question your own assumptions. Do you judge others by their faith, accent, or political belief? Now imagine a world where we look beyond those boundaries. A world where we face challenges together, share burdens fairly, and thrive as one. That world is not a fantasy. It is a choice. One we must make, again and again.

The stakes could not be higher. Our planet and our future depend on it. So the final question remains: Will we continue chasing shadows, or will we finally build a world guided by reason?

DESCRIPTION

Across the natural world, conflict is a fundamental feature of life. Lions fiercely guard their territories, dogs snarl at intruders from neighbouring packs, and birds squabble over scraps of food, even among their own kind. These instincts, rooted in survival, competition, and the drive to secure resources, reveal a universal truth: division and rivalry are not unique to humans. Yet unlike other species, humans possess the remarkable ability to reflect, reason, and rise above these primal urges. Despite this capacity, we remain deeply fractured.

On a single planet, sustained by the same air, water, and sunlight, humanity has divided itself into 195 nations, each with its own borders, laws, and identities. Within these nations, countless regions, states, and communities further fragment us, often fostering mistrust or hostility toward those considered different. These divisions are not only geographic; they are reinforced by religion, politics, and regional identities that shape our beliefs, values, and allegiances.

Historically, human conflict has often stemmed from the ambition to dominate or reshape others. Kings and emperors, from Alexander the Great to colonial powers, conquered lands, altered cultures, and redrew maps, leaving behind legacies of resentment and division. Whether through religious wars, territorial disputes, or political ideologies, these interventions planted seeds of discord that continue to grow. The Crusades pitted Christians against Muslims. The partition of India split Hindus and Muslims apart. The Cold War divided the world between capitalism and communism. These examples show how religion, geography, and political beliefs have long served as fuel for conflict, often tapping into our tribal instincts to turn people against one another.

Yet the same intellect that enables humans to build civilizations also gives us the tools to overcome these divisions. By recognizing our shared biology, shared environment, and shared ability to reason, we can move toward unity. This book argues that our survival and progress rely on choosing rational thought over fear, blind belief, or the hunger for power. Through historical reflection and a hopeful vision for the future, **Divided We Stand: Reason Over Religion, Region, and Politics** explores why we fight, what we lose, and how we can move forward together.

11 | Description

CHAPTER 1

THE ROOTS OF CONFLICT: LESSONS FROM NATURE AND HUMANITY

Overview

In the vast complexity of life on Earth, conflict is constant. From the snarling standoffs of wolves defending their pack's territory to the frantic squabbles of sparrows over a crust of bread, the natural world is a stage for rivalry, competition, and division. These struggles, driven by the primal imperatives of survival such as securing food, shelter, or mates, are not mere chaos but the predictable outcomes of biology shaping behaviour. Animals mark boundaries, assert dominance, and protect their kin, not out of malice but because evolution has programmed them to prioritize their own survival and that of their group.

Humans, however, are not just another species bound by instinct. We breathe the same air, drink from the same rivers, and walk the same earth, yet we fracture our world into 195 nations, countless regions, and a multitude of ideologies. Each of these is guarded with the same intensity as a lion defending its pride. Our conflicts, whether over land, faith, or power, mirror the territorial disputes and resource struggles of the animal kingdom, but they are amplified by our imagination, memory, and ambition. Unlike wolves or sparrows, we possess self-awareness and reason, abilities that allow us to reflect on our behaviour and imagine a better way. Yet sadly, we often choose division instead of unity and rivalry instead of cooperation.

This chapter explores the origins of conflict, tracing its roots from the instincts embedded in our biology to the complex societies we have constructed on top of those instincts. By examining how both animals and humans draw boundaries between territories, packs, or nations, we begin to understand why division often feels natural, even inevitable. Evolutionary psychology shows how survival instincts influence our sense of group identity, encouraging loyalty to those we see as part of "us" and suspicion toward those we label as "them." The idea of in-groups and out-groups helps explain why we stand behind flags, faiths, or tribes, sometimes to the point of violence. But because we have the power to reason, humanity's continued engagement in conflict becomes both a mystery and an opportunity. This chapter asks the central question of this book: Why do we continue to divide ourselves, even though we share the same needs and the same potential for cooperation? In seeking the answer, we begin a journey through religion, region, and politics, with the goal of building a rational case for unity.

- **Core Insights with Depth**

1. Animals mark territories and compete for resources, paralleling human borders and wars

In the African savanna, a lion's roar reverberates across the plains, not as a song but as a warning: this land is mine. The pride's territory, marked by scent and defended with claws, ensures access to prey and safety for cubs. Similarly, a pack of hyenas will drive off intruders with relentless aggression, their survival depending on exclusive control of hunting grounds. Birds also stake claims. For instance, a robin will fiercely chase away rivals from its nesting site, refusing to share even when food is abundant. These behaviours are not random. They are evolutionary strategies designed to secure limited resources in a world governed by competition.

Humans reflect these instincts, though our battlegrounds are much larger and our methods far more advanced. Consider the Great Wall of China, which stretches thousands of miles to mark the boundary of an empire, or modern border fences equipped with sensors and patrolled by armed guards. Nations, like animal territories, are defined by boundaries. Some follow natural features like rivers, while others are artificially drawn on maps. All are defended with determination. Wars, whether ancient or modern, often center on the control of vital resources such as land, oil, water, or trade routes. The Peloponnesian War between Athens and Sparta was largely a struggle for dominance over Greek territory and trade, much like wolves competing for prime hunting grounds. In our own time, disputes over regions like the South China Sea reveal how nations continue to clash over access to maritime wealth, echoing ancient patterns of survival-based rivalry.

However, human conflict extends far beyond the pursuit of resources. Our borders are not only physical. They are also ideological, cultural, and deeply emotional. We do not fight only for land. We fight to defend our beliefs, our identities, and our sense of who we are. This shift from basic instinct to complex identity sets the foundation for understanding how our biology influences division, and more importantly, how we might evolve beyond it.

2. Humanity's unique capacity for self-awareness and reason makes conflict tragic and solvable

Unlike lions or robins, humans can step back from their instincts. A wolf cannot question why it growls at a rival pack; it simply acts. But humans, endowed with self-awareness, can ask: Why do I fear this stranger? Why do I cling to this flag? Our ability to reflect allows us to see ourselves as part of a larger whole, a species sharing one fragile planet. Reason, born from this awareness, lets us analyze causes, predict consequences, and imagine alternatives. We have built telescopes to peer into distant galaxies and created vaccines to conquer diseases, accomplishments no other creature could begin to imagine.

Yet this gift makes our conflicts even more tragic. When we wage wars, exclude others, or hoard resources, we do so with full awareness of the suffering we cause. The Rwandan Genocide in 1994, where neighbours turned on neighbours, was not a blind instinctual clash but a calculated descent into hatred, driven by propaganda and fear. Our reason, which could have been used to build peace, was instead twisted to deepen division. This contradiction between our capacity for destruction and our power to create defines the human condition.

But within every tragedy lies a seed of hope. If reason can be hijacked by fear or greed, it can also be reclaimed for unity. The same minds that designed weapons have also drafted peace treaties. One example is the Camp David Accords of 1978, which helped ease tensions between Egypt and Israel through dialogue. Our self-awareness allows us to challenge old habits, question tribal loyalties, and imagine a world where cooperation replaces rivalry. This potential is at the heart of this book's message. We have the power to choose a better path if we are willing to think.

3. The central question: Why do we divide ourselves despite shared needs and cooperation's potential?

Every human, regardless of nation or creed, seeks the same essentials: food, safety, connection. We all recoil from pain, cherish our families, and dream of a better future. Our biology unites us. Our DNA is 99.9 percent identical, and our bodies are sustained by the same oxygen and water. A child in Tokyo and a child in Timbuktu laugh with the same joy and cry with the same tears. On a finite planet, our fates are intertwined. A drought in one region ripples through global markets, and a virus in one city spreads to all. Cooperation, not conflict, aligns with our shared needs.

Yet, we divide ourselves relentlessly. We build walls, both literal, like the U.S. and Mexico border, and figurative, like the silence between feuding communities. We hoard resources, as nations stockpile wealth while others starve, mirroring ants guarding their colony's stores. Why? If survival demands collaboration, why do we cling to separation? This question is not just philosophical. It is urgent. Climate change, pandemics, and technological risks such as unchecked artificial intelligence demand global unity, yet we continue to waste energy on old rivalries.

The answer lies partly in our past, in instincts that once helped us survive but now collide with the realities of a deeply interconnected world. By exploring these roots, this chapter begins a journey through religion, region, and politics, the lenses through which we often intensify division. But it also plants a seed of hope. If we understand why we divide, we can choose to unite and use reason to rewrite our story.

- **Outlined Viewpoint**

1. Evolutionary psychology: How survival instincts shape group identity

Evolutionary psychology offers a lens to understand why division feels so natural. Millions of years ago, our ancestors survived by banding together in small groups such as families, tribes, and clans. These groups provided safety from predators, shared labour for hunting, and protection against rival bands. Loyalty to the group was paramount. Outsiders, who might steal resources or bring disease, were viewed with suspicion. This instinct, hardwired through generations, birthed group identity: a sense of "us" defined by shared traits such as language, appearance, or customs.

Fast forward to today, and these instincts manifest in nationalism, where citizens rally around flags, or in cultural pride, where traditions become badges of belonging. Evolutionary psychologists like Robert Kurzban argue that our brains are primed to categorize people into groups, often exaggerating differences to reinforce the divide between "us" and "them." This explains why sports fans may riot over team rivalries or why ethnic tensions flare in diverse societies. The 1990s Los Angeles riots, sparked by racial divides, showed how quickly group identity can ignite violence, even in a modern city.

But evolution is not destiny. Our ancestors also cooperated across groups by trading goods and sharing knowledge to survive. The Silk Road, linking ancient China to Europe, thrived because merchants transcended tribal lines for mutual gain. Today, our globalized world demands this cooperation on a grand scale. By understanding how survival instincts shape identity, we can see division as a default rather than a mandate, and we can use reason to rise above it.

2. In-Group vs. Out-Group dynamics

At the heart of conflict lies a simple mechanism: in-group versus out-group dynamics. Social psychologists like Henri Tajfel have shown that humans instinctively favour their own group, those who share their beliefs, looks, or goals, while distrusting outsiders. This bias, called "social identity theory," emerges even in trivial settings. In Tajfel's experiments, people assigned to random groups, such as a "blue team" and a "red team," quickly showed favouritism, rewarding their own at others' expense.

In nature, this dynamic is clear. A chimpanzee troop will attack outsiders to protect its food or mates, strengthening bonds within the group. Humans amplify this instinct through culture. Consider medieval Europe, where Christian villagers viewed Jewish neighbours as outsiders, fueling pogroms despite their shared humanity. Or look at modern politics, where partisan tribes like Democrats and Republicans, Labour and Conservatives, NDA and INDI Alliance demonize one another, often ignoring common goals such as prosperity and safety.

These dynamics are not just psychological; they are also exploited. Leaders stoke fear of the other to unify their base, as Hitler did with anti-Semitism or as colonial powers did by pitting African tribes against one another. The Rwandan Genocide serves as a grim example. Hutu radio broadcasts branded Tutsis as cockroaches, dehumanizing them to justify slaughter. Yet in-group loyalty can also inspire good. Think of communities rallying together after disasters. The challenge is to redirect this instinct toward a broader in-group: humanity itself. Reason allows us to redefine "us" to include everyone, as movements like the Red Cross demonstrate by aiding strangers across borders.

CHAPTER 2

RELIGION:

FAITH AS A DIVIDER AND UNIFIER

Overview

Religion, at its core, is humanity's attempt to grapple with life's deepest questions: Why are we here? What happens after death? How should we live? Across millennia, faiths such as Christianity, Hinduism, Islam, Buddhism, and countless others have offered answers, interlacing communities together with shared rituals, moral codes, and visions of the divine. A church's hymns, a mosque's call to prayer, or a temple's flickering lamps can bind people in a sense of belonging that transcends the mundane. For billions, religion is a wellspring of meaning, inspiring acts of dharma and karma, charity, art, and sacrifice.

Yet, this same force of unity often sows division. When religious differences are weaponized by zealots, rulers, or mobs, faith becomes a banner for conflict. The very texts that preach love can be twisted to justify hate; the communities that offer solace can exclude those who believe differently. Religion's power to forge strong group identities makes it a double-edged sword. It unites "us" but can vilify "them." Historically, this tension has fueled wars, persecutions, and partitions, leaving scars that linger across generations. From the blood-soaked Crusades to the fractured legacy of India's partition, religious fervor has often intertwined with politics and regional ambitions, amplifying strife.

But religion's story is not solely one of division. It has also inspired peace, reconciliation, and cooperation, from interfaith dialogues to movements for justice. This chapter examines religion's dual role, exploring how it divides when doctrines are rigid or exploited, and unites when it appeals to shared humanity. By analyzing historical conflicts like the Crusades, the Thirty Years' War, and the Partition of India, we see how faith has been a spark for violence, but also how it can light the way toward healing. Ultimately, this chapter argues that religion's impact depends on human choices: to wield it as a weapon or a bridge. Through reason, we can amplify its unifying potential, a theme that foreshadows this book's call to transcend division.

- **Core Insights with Depth**

1. Religions create strong In-Group identities, leading to exclusion or hostility

Religion's ability to unite is rooted in its creation of in-group identities, shared beliefs and practices that make adherents feel part of something larger. A Catholic kneeling at Mass, a Muslim fasting during Ramadan, or a Hindu offering prayers at a festival feels connected to millions sharing the same rituals. This bond, social psychologists like Jonathan Haidt argue, taps into our evolutionary need for group cohesion, fostering trust and cooperation within the faith community. Sanatan Dharma's concept of *daan and seva*, medieval monasteries that sheltered the poor, Islamic *zakat* for the needy, and Sikh *langars* that feed all comers all illustrate how in-group loyalty can inspire acts of goodness.

But this strength becomes a weakness when the in-group defines itself against an out-group. The tighter the bond within, the sharper the divide without. Early Christians faced Roman persecution, cementing their identity as distinct from pagans; centuries later, they turned the tables, marginalizing non-Christians. In medieval Spain, the Reconquista rallied Christians against Muslims and Jews, culminating in expulsions and forced conversions. This exclusionary impulse persists. In Myanmar, Buddhist nationalists have targeted Tamils and Muslims, claiming to protect their faith's dominance. When "us" versus "them" hardens, religion does not just unite; it alienates, breeding suspicion or outright hostility.

The danger lies in absolutism. When believers see their faith as the sole truth, others become not just different but wrong, even demonic. This mindset fueled witch hunts, where dissenters were branded heretics, and modern sectarian violence, like Sunni Shia clashes in Iraq. Yet, these dynamics are not unique to religion. They echo the tribal instincts from Chapter 1. Religion amplifies them, giving cosmic stakes to human rivalries. Understanding this helps us see division as a human choice, not a divine mandate.

2. Conflicts arise when doctrines are interpreted rigidly or used to justify power grabs

Religious texts, whether the Vedas, Quran, or the Bible, are vast and complex, open to myriad interpretations. A single verse can inspire mercy or militancy, depending on who wields it. Rigid readings that insist on literal or exclusive truth often ignite conflict. In the 16th century, Protestant reformers like Martin Luther challenged Catholic authority by citing scripture. The Catholic Church responded with excommunications, branding dissenters as threats to salvation. This clash of dogmas did not just spark debate; it set Europe ablaze.

Worse, religion becomes a tool for power when leaders cloak ambition in holy rhetoric. Kings, clerics, and warlords have long used faith to rally followers, justifying conquest or control. The Catholic Church's indulgences, selling forgiveness for profit, provoked the Reformation, blending spiritual corruption with economic greed. In modern times, groups like ISIS invoke Islam to legitimize violence, ignoring the Quran's calls for mercy, such as Surah Al-Anfal 8.61, which urges peace if enemies incline toward it. These distortions are not about faith alone; they are about power dressed in sacred garb.

Such conflicts reveal a pattern: rigid doctrine narrows reason, while power hungry leaders exploit belief to divide. Yet this is not inevitable. Every faith has voices of moderation. Think of Sufi poets like Rumi, who saw divinity in all humanity. By choosing flexible and inclusive interpretations, believers can defuse conflict, a point we will revisit in the chapter's hopeful examples.

3. Moments where religion inspires peace or cooperation show Its potential for good

Religion's divisive legacy is only half the story. At its best, faith transcends boundaries, uniting people across divides. The same texts used to wage war can call for peace. The Mahabharata declares *"Ahimsa paramo dharmah,"* meaning nonviolence is the highest duty. Christianity's Sermon on the Mount urges love for enemies (Matthew 5:44). Islam's Hadith praises those who show kindness to all (Sahih Muslim 2319). Buddhism's Dhammapada advocates nonviolence (verse 5). These ideals have fueled movements that heal rather than harm.

Consider the role of faith in the American Civil Rights Movement during the 1950s and 1960s. Martin Luther King Jr., a Baptist pastor, drew on Christian teachings of justice and love to challenge racial segregation, uniting Black and White allies in a moral cause. His "I Have a Dream" speech invoked universal dignity, rooted in faith, to bridge divides. Similarly, in South Africa, Archbishop Desmond Tutu's Anglican faith guided the Truth and Reconciliation Commission from 1996 to 2003, fostering forgiveness after apartheid's horrors. These examples show religion as a unifier when it emphasizes shared humanity over dogma.

Even across faiths, cooperation shines. The 13th century meeting between St. Francis of Assisi and Sultan Al Kamil during the Crusades, two men of different religions sharing respectful dialogue, offers a glimpse of what is possible. Today, interfaith initiatives like the Parliament of the World's Religions, founded in 1893 and still ongoing, bring thousands together to tackle global issues like poverty and climate change. These moments prove religion can be a force for good, aligning with the book's call for reason driven unity.

- **Historical Examples with Detail**

1. The Crusades (11th–13th Centuries)

The Crusades were a series of holy wars launched by European Christians to seize Jerusalem and other Holy Land sites from Muslim control. Sparked by Pope Urban II's 1095 call at Clermont, they blended religious zeal through promises of salvation for warriors with political ambition, as kings and nobles sought land and glory. The First Crusade, from 1096 to 1099, captured Jerusalem, but at horrific cost: massacres of Muslims, Jews, and even Christians left streets bloodied. Later crusades, such as the Fourth in 1204, saw Christians sacking Christian Constantinople, exposing the greed beneath the rhetoric.

The fallout was profound. Muslims, under leaders like Saladin, rallied to reclaim territory, deepening mistrust.

Stereotypes of Christians as barbaric invaders and Muslims as infidels took root, echoing in modern tensions, such as debates over Islamophobia. Yet, the Crusades also had moments of unity. Saladin's chivalrous treatment of captives and trade between faiths during truces showed humanity persisting amid conflict. This duality underscores how faith, when rigid, divides, but when humane, connects.

2. The Thirty Years' War (1618–1648)

Europe's Thirty Years' War began as a religious clash between Catholics and Protestants in the Holy Roman Empire, ignited by the Defenestration of Prague (1618), when Protestant nobles rebelled against Catholic rule. What started as a doctrinal dispute over issues like papal authority spiralled into a continent wide struggle, as powers like France, Sweden, and Spain pursued territorial and political gains. Armies ravaged villages, famine spread, and up to 8 million died, making it one of Europe's deadliest conflicts before the 20th century.

Religion was the spark, but politics fanned the flames. Catholic France backed Protestant allies to weaken rivals, showing how faith was often a pretext. The Peace of Westphalia (1648) ended the war, granting religious tolerance and state sovereignty, a rational step toward coexistence. This historical resolution echoes the central message of this book: reason can temper faith's excesses, forging unity from chaos.

3. The Partition of India (1947)

When British India gained independence in 1947, colonial policies and rising Hindu Muslim tensions led to its division into India (Hindu majority) and

Pakistan (Muslim majority). Religion wasn't the sole driver; economic and political rivalries, stoked by Britain's "divide and rule" tactics, played a role, but it became the rallying cry. Communal riots erupted, with mobs targeting neighbours based on faith. Up to 15 million were displaced, and 1 to 2 million died in the ensuing violence, one of the largest forced migrations in history.

The partition's legacy, hostility between India and Pakistan, including wars (1947, 1965, 1971) and ongoing disputes, shows how religious identity, once weaponized, entrenches division. Yet, figures like Mahatma Gandhi, who stood for nonviolence and interfaith harmony, devoted their lives to bridging these divides, even fasting to calm communal unrest. His assassination in 1948 by a member of his own community reflects the tragic cost of intolerance. And yet, his legacy reminds us that when guided by compassion and reason, faith can become a force for unity.

- **Outlined Viewpoint**

1. How religious texts are interpreted to justify war and peace

Sacred texts are like prisms, reflecting the reader's intent. The Bible's "eye for an eye" (Exodus 21:24) was cited by medieval inquisitors to punish heretics, yet Jesus's call to "turn the other cheek" (Matthew 5:39) inspired pacifists like Quaker abolitionists. The Quran's verses on jihad (e.g., Surah Al Baqarah 2:191) are cherry picked by extremists to justify violence, but its emphasis on mercy (Surah Al Rahman) guides charities like relief. Hindu texts like the Bhagavad Gita depict war as duty (Krishna's advice to Arjuna), yet its spiritual depth has also been a source of inspiration for peace and reflection.

Interpretation hinges on context and choice. Medieval clerics ignored inconvenient verses to rally crusaders; modern theologians highlight them to build bridges. The 1993 Oslo Accords, where religious leaders supported Israeli Palestinian talks, showed texts bending toward peace when reason prevails. This fluidity means religion's impact, divisive or unifying, rests on human agency.

2. Modern examples like interfaith dialogues to foreshadow unity

Today, religion's unifying potential shines in interfaith efforts. The United Religions Initiative, founded in 2000, connects thousands across faiths to address issues like refugee aid and climate justice. In Jordan, the 2004 Amman Message united Sunni and Shia scholars to denounce extremism, affirming Islam's diversity. After the 2001 attacks in New York, interfaith vigils where Christians, Muslims, and Jews prayed together helped rebuild community amid fear.

These initiatives succeed because they emphasize shared human values such as compassion, justice, and dignity rather than strict doctrinal boundaries. They reflect the central vision of this book, which is that reason and empathy can guide faith toward cooperation instead of conflict.

3. How religion intersects with politics or region to amplify conflict

Religion rarely acts alone; it becomes a force multiplier when entangled with politics or regional identity. In the Crusades, popes and kings used faith to legitimize territorial conquests, blending spiritual authority with political ambition. The Thirty Years' War saw emperors invoke Catholicism to maintain control over fractious regions, while

Protestant princes resisted to assert their autonomy.

In India's partition, British colonial policies deepened Hindu Muslim divides, setting the stage for mass polarization. Local leaders, too, exploited religious sentiments for political leverage, most notably Mohammad Ali Jinnah, whose demand for a separate Muslim state played a decisive role in framing India's division along religious lines. What followed was one of the largest and bloodiest migrations in human history.

Modern examples echo this pattern. In Northern Ireland (1960s to 1998), the Catholic Protestant "Troubles" were as much about regional identity and political control as religious doctrine, claiming over 3,500 lives before the Good Friday Agreement. In the Middle East, Iran's Shia theocracy and Saudi Arabia's Sunni monarchy vie for dominance, cloaking geopolitical rivalry in the language of faith.

These intersections reveal why religion can divide so deeply: it is a powerful symbol, easily hijacked by worldly agendas. Untangling it demands reason, empathy, and the ability to distinguish spiritual conviction from political manipulation.

CHAPTER 3

REGION:

TERRITORY AND IDENTITY

Overview

The earth's surface, a seamless expanse of mountains, rivers, and plains, bears no natural lines dividing one people from another. Yet, humans have etched borders across it, some carved by geography, others drawn by whim or conquest. These lines, whether marking nations, regions, or neighbourhoods, are more than cartographic fictions; they shape how we see ourselves and others. A passport declares your nation, a dialect ties you to a province, a street sign roots you to a community. These regional identities can inspire pride, preserve culture, and foster belonging, much like the religious bonds explored in Chapter 2. But they also ignite conflict when they exclude, provoke rivalry, or stake competing claims to the same soil.

Borders, though human made, command fierce loyalty, often at the cost of blood. A flag planted on a hilltop or a fence slicing through a desert isn't just a marker; it's a declaration of "us" against "them," echoing the in-group dynamics of biology and faith. Territorial disputes, from global wars to local turf battles, reveal how deeply we tie identity to place. Yet, these conflicts often mask deeper issues: competition for resources like water or oil, or grievances rooted in history's long shadow. The Rwandan Genocide, the Israeli Palestinian conflict, and the Yugoslav Wars illustrate how regional identities, ethnic, national, or local, can spiral into violence when fueled by fear or ambition.

Let us explore why geography divides us, tracing the roots of territorial conflict to human constructs and decisions. We will examine how colonialism's arbitrary maps sowed discord, how migration and globalization strain regional identities, and how cooperation such as the example of the European Union offers a powerful counterpoint. Building on the instincts (Chapter 1) and beliefs (Chapter 2) that fragment us, this chapter reveals how regions, like religions, are tools of human imagination, capable of uniting or destroying, depending on how we wield them. By recognizing their influence, we take a step closer to the rational unity this book aims to illuminate.

- **Core Insights with Depth**

1. Borders are human constructs, yet inspire fierce loyalty and violence

Borders are inventions, as artificial as the lines on a child's drawing. Some follow rivers or ridges, but many, such as the straight-edged frontiers slicing through Africa or the Middle East, were sketched by diplomats with little regard for the people they divided. The 1884 Berlin Conference, where European powers carved up Africa, created nations like Nigeria or Kenya with no basis in local realities. Yet these lines harden into truths. Citizens salute flags, soldiers guard checkpoints, and wars erupt to shift a boundary by mere miles.

This loyalty stems from what geographer Yi-Fu Tuan calls "place attachment," the emotional bond to the land we call home. A villager in Kashmir or a city dweller in Belfast does not just live somewhere; their identity is woven into the soil, streets, or stories of that place. When borders are threatened, so is selfhood. The 1969 Sino-Soviet border clashes, where hundreds died over desolate Ussuri River islands, were not about the land's value but about pride and dominance. Similarly, urban gang wars like those between Los Angeles' Bloods and Crips turn neighbourhoods into mini nations, with youth dying for streets they claim as theirs.

The tragedy is that borders, being constructs, do not need to divide. They could be bridges, as trade routes like the ancient Silk Road once were. But when loyalty to place overrides reason, violence follows. This pattern appears in Rwanda, in the Israeli and Palestinian conflict, and in the wars of former Yugoslavia. This point connects back to the evolutionary instincts discussed in Chapter 1. Our territorial nature, like a lion's, is primal, but our ability to rethink it is uniquely human.

2. Regional identities foster pride but also exclusion

Regional identities, shaped by ethnicity, language, or culture, give life its richness. A Catalan's pride in their language, a Zulu's reverence for ancestral traditions, or a Texan's swagger all root people in something larger than themselves. These identities preserve history: Scotland's bagpipes, Bengal's poetry, or Ethiopia's ancient churches carry centuries of meaning. Like religion's in-groups, they unite through shared symbols, strengthening resilience against hardship.

But pride can curdle into exclusion. When regional identity demands purity or superiority, it shuts out others. In Sri Lanka, Sinhalese nationalism, tied to language and Buddhist heritage, marginalized Tamils, sparking a civil war (1983 to 2009) that killed over 100,000. Similarly, Quebec's French-speaking identity, while culturally vibrant, has at times alienated English speakers, fueling separatist tensions. In India, recent waves of resistance in South Indian states, particularly Tamil Nadu and Karnataka, highlight how linguistic pride can spark opposition to perceived cultural domination. The pushback against Hindi imposition is not just about language; it is a defense of regional identity, a stand against homogenization under the guise of national unity. Exclusion becomes deadly when "our" region claims moral or historical supremacy, casting outsiders as threats. The Nazi myth of Aryan homeland justified genocide, showing how regional pride, untethered from reason, turns toxic.

This duality mirrors Chapter 2's religious tensions: identity unites within but divides without. The challenge is balancing pride with openness, a balance possible only through rational reflection, as later examples of cooperation will show.

3. Territorial disputes mask deeper issues like resource competition or historical grievances

On the surface, territorial conflicts are about land, who owns it, who belongs there. But dig deeper, and they often hide struggles for power, wealth, or retribution. Resources drive many disputes: the Nile River's waters pit Egypt against upstream Ethiopia, threatening conflict as dams shift flows. The Arctic, once ice locked, now sees Russia, Canada, and others vying for oil and shipping routes as glaciers melt. These echo Chapter 1's animal rivalries, wolves fighting for hunting grounds, but with human stakes magnified.

Historical grievances add fuel. A border drawn decades ago, a village razed, or a people displaced can fester, turning geography into a scorecard of past wrongs. The India-China border clash in 1962, rooted in colonial era maps, still sparks skirmishes, with each side nursing old slights. Similarly, local disputes like Northern Ireland's Catholic and Protestant neighbourhoods carry centuries of memory, where a mural or flag reignites vendettas.

These layers show why territorial conflicts persist: land is a symbol, not just soil. Resolving them demands addressing root causes, poverty, inequity, or unhealed wounds, through dialogue and reason, not just redrawing lines. The historical cases below reveal this complexity, while cooperative examples point to solutions.

Historical Examples with Detail

1. The Rwandan Genocide (1994)

In 100 days, Rwanda descended into horror as Hutu extremists slaughtered nearly 800,000 Tutsis and moderate Hutus. The roots lay in regional identity twisted by history. Hutus and Tutsis, sharing language and land, were divided by colonial powers, Germans, then Belgians, who favoured Tutsis as a ruling class, creating an ethnic hierarchy. Arbitrary ID cards labeled people, hardening fluid identities into rigid categories. When Belgium withdrew in 1962, power flipped to Hutus, who nursed resentment from decades of subjugation.

By 1994, economic woes and political propaganda, radio broadcasts calling Tutsis "cockroaches," ignited genocide. Neighbours killed neighbours with machetes, churches became killing grounds, and rivers choked with bodies. The region's borders, drawn by outsiders, trapped these groups together, amplifying local grudges into catastrophe. Post genocide, Rwanda's government banned ethnic labels, pushing a unified "Rwandan" identity, an imperfect and late but rational step toward healing. This case shows how colonial borders and regional identities, when exploited, turn geography into a graveyard.

2. The Israeli-Palestinian conflict (20th century–present)

Few disputes embody territorial conflict like that between Israelis and Palestinians. Both claim the same land: modern Israel, the West Bank, and Gaza, rooted in deep historical and religious ties. For Jews, it is the scriptural promised land, a refuge after centuries of persecution, formalized by the 1948 creation of Israel.

For Palestinians, it is their ancestral home, where families farmed for generations, shattered by displacement during Israel's founding, known as the Nakba.

The conflict's toll is staggering. Wars in 1948, 1967, and 1973, along with intifadas and ongoing violence, have killed tens of thousands, with millions displaced or living under occupation. Borders continue to shift as Israeli settlements expand and Gaza's walls grow tighter. Yet peace talks, such as the Oslo Accords of 1993, often falter over the question of control.

In October 2023, Hamas launched a surprise and brutal attack on southern Israel, killing civilians and taking hostages. The attack led to widespread shock and condemnation. Israel responded with overwhelming force, launching airstrikes and a ground invasion in Gaza, aiming to dismantle Hamas's infrastructure. The escalation caused severe humanitarian consequences, with thousands of casualties and widespread displacement on both sides.

Religion, as discussed in Chapter 2, fuels passion, but the core of the conflict lies in the land itself. Two peoples claim the same territory. Competition over resources such as water and farmland, along with grievances over expulsions and terrorism, deepens the stalemate. Yet grassroots efforts like the Parents Circle, which unites bereaved Israeli and Palestinian families, offer glimpses of empathy. This case shows how territorial identity, tied to survival, resists reason but still yearns for resolution.

3. The Yugoslav wars (1991–2001)

When Yugoslavia unravelled after the Cold War, its diverse regions, home to Serbs, Croats, Bosniaks, and others, became battlegrounds. Unified under Tito's socialism, the country fractured as nationalism surged. Each group claimed historic rights to land: Serbs saw Bosnia as theirs, Croats sought autonomy, Bosniaks defended multiethnic Sarajevo. The wars in Croatia (1991 to 1995), Bosnia (1992 to 1995), and Kosovo (1998 to 1999) killed 140,000 and displaced millions. Srebrenica's 1995 massacre, where 8,000 Bosniak men and boys died, marked the nadir of ethnic cleansing.

Borders were both cause and prize. Serbia's Milosevic stoked territorial dreams of a "Greater Serbia," while Croatia's Tudjman mirrored the tactic. Historical grudges, such as Ottoman rule and World War II massacres, fueled propaganda, turning neighbours into enemies. The Dayton Accords of 1995 redrew Bosnia's map, halting violence but freezing ethnic divides. Yugoslavia shows how regional identity, when weaponized, shatters coexistence, yet negotiated borders, however flawed, can pause the cycle.

- **Outlined Viewpoint**

1. Colonialism's redrawn maps sowing discord

Colonialism reshaped the world's geography, often with devastating consequences. In Africa, the 1884–1885 Berlin Conference divided the continent among European powers, ignoring ethnic, linguistic, or cultural realities. Nigeria alone blends over 250 ethnic groups, with Hausa, Yoruba, and Igbo regions clashing over power post-independence (1960). The Biafra War (1967–1970), where Igbo secessionists fought a federal government, killed 1–3 million, rooted in these artificial borders.

The Middle East fared no better. The 1916 Sykes-Picot Agreement carved up Ottoman lands into British and French zones, creating Iraq and Syria with no regard for Sunni, Shia, or Kurdish identities. These lines bred instability as ISIS exploited Iraq's sectarian divides in 2014, claiming a "caliphate" to erase colonial borders. Colonial maps were not just lines; they were time bombs, embedding regional tensions that erupt when power shifts. Understanding this history reveals why borders spark conflict and why rational redrawing or cooperation matter.

2. Migration and Globalization challenging regional identities

Today's world moves faster than ever, with migration and globalization blurring regional lines. In Europe, African and Middle Eastern migrants spark debates over "national identity," fueling far-right movements like Germany's AfD or France's National Rally. In the U.S., Latino immigration reshapes states like Texas, where Anglo and Hispanic identities vie for cultural dominance. These shifts threaten regional pride, as newcomers challenge "who belongs."

Globalization adds pressure. Global brands, English as a lingua franca, and digital culture erode local distinctions as Breton farmers or Appalachian coal miners feel their uniqueness fading. This breeds backlash: Catalonia's 2017 independence push or Scotland's Brexit era separatism reflect regions clinging to identity against a homogenizing world. Yet, migration also enriches as London's diversity drives its economy, and Silicon Valley thrives on global talent. The tension shows regional identity evolving, requiring reason to balance tradition with inclusion.

3. Successful regional cooperation as a counterpoint

If regions divide, they can also unite. The European Union, born from World War II's ashes, is a testament. In 1951, France, Germany, and others pooled coal and steel, resources once fueling wars, under the European Coal and Steel Community. Today, 27 nations share trade, laws, and a currency, with open borders easing old rivalries. The EU isn't perfect; Brexit (2016) exposed cracks, but it slashed conflict's odds, making war between France and Germany unthinkable.

Elsewhere, regional cooperation offers hope. ASEAN, established in 1967, connects Southeast Asian nations and has helped ease tensions over contested borders, such as those between Thailand and Cambodia. Even at a local level, twin cities like Minneapolis and St. Paul or Buda and Pest illustrate how formerly divided regions can unite for mutual benefit. These examples show that when reason takes precedence over pride, borders can soften and identities can converge. They align with this book's central vision: geography need not divide us if we choose to redefine its meaning through cooperation and shared purpose.

With that foundation, we now turn to Chapter 4: Politics, Power, and Ideology. This chapter examines how political systems—monarchies, democracies, communism, fascism—and ideological frameworks fracture societies when they elevate power, dogma, or fear above shared humanity. Building on the instincts, beliefs, and regions that divide us, this chapter explores how politics manipulates these forces to sustain control. Through historical case studies, modern polarization, propaganda's influence, and moments of compromise, it advances the book's core argument: that rational unity is possible, but only when we confront the mechanisms that exploit our divisions.

CHAPTER 4

POLITICS: POWER AND IDEOLOGY

Overview

Politics, at its best, is humanity's attempt to organize societies for the common good: to allocate resources, uphold justice, and secure peace. From ancient tribal councils to modern parliaments, it promises order amid chaos. Yet, politics often betrays this promise, becoming a battleground where power and ideology trump shared humanity. Monarchies crown divine right kings, democracies pit factions against each other, communism demands class warfare, and fascism glorifies the state over the individual. Each system, whatever its ideals, can divide when it prioritizes control or dogma over connection.

Like religion and region, politics exploits our instinctual divides, amplifying differences in faith or geography to rally loyalty. It draws lines not just on maps but in minds, casting opponents as enemies rather than fellow humans. Leaders wield fear, conjuring "others" to unite followers, while ideological crusades such as capitalism versus communism or liberalism versus authoritarianism split the globe into camps. The Cold War's shadow looms large here, as do the French Revolution's chaos and Nigeria's civil war, each showing how politics can destabilize when it loses sight of reason.

But politics isn't doomed to divide. Moments of compromise, like South Africa's post-apartheid transition, reveal its potential to heal. This chapter analyzes how political systems and ideologies fracture societies, exploring their manipulation of fear, their reliance on propaganda, and their echoes in today's polarized world. Building on the tribal instincts, sacred loyalties and territorial pride that shape conflict, it argues that politics, like all human constructs, can be redirected toward unity if we choose reason over rivalry. By dissecting its failures and possibilities, we move closer to transcending the divisions this book seeks to overcome.

- **Core Insights with Depth**

1. Politics exploits religious or regional differences to consolidate power

Politics thrives on division, often hijacking the fault lines of religion and region to cement authority. A leader facing unrest can rally support by invoking faith or homeland, turning abstract governance into a visceral cause. In medieval Europe, monarchs claimed divine right, fusing politics with religion to justify rule. England's Henry VIII broke with Rome to control both church and state. Today, politicians stoke regional pride. In India, the BJP often emphasizes cultural and religious heritage, drawing on Hindu identity as a unifying force, while Scotland's SNP frames independence as an expression of cultural self-determination.

This tactic isn't just opportunistic; it's strategic. By amplifying existing divides, leaders create loyal "in-groups" while marginalizing "out-groups." Iran's 1979 Islamic Revolution blended Shia identity with anti-Western politics, consolidating power by demonizing the U.S. as the "Great Satan." Similarly, Rwanda's pre-genocide leaders used ethnic radio to pit Hutus against Tutsis, securing political control through fear. These examples echo Chapter 1's evolutionary psychology: politics exploits our tribal wiring, making division feel natural. But this manipulation thrives only when reason is absent, a vulnerability we can counter.

2. Ideological battles create global fault lines

If religion offers cosmic truths and regions anchor identity, ideologies are politics' blueprints for utopia or dystopia. Capitalism champions markets, communism demands equality, fascism exalts the nation, and democracy prizes choice. Each carries a vision, but when absolutized, they clash, carving the world into opposing camps. The 20th century's ideological wars between capitalism and communism, and between democracy and fascism, were not just debates; they were global ruptures, costing millions of lives.

These battles transcend borders, turning local disputes into proxy fights. The Spanish Civil War (1936 to 1939) pitted communists and anarchists against fascists, drawing Soviet and Nazi support, a microcosm of Europe's ideological split. After World War II, the Iron Curtain divided East from West, not just geographically but philosophically. Berlin's Wall was not made of bricks alone but symbolized a clash of visions. Even today, democracy's decline in places like Hungary or Turkey reflects ideological tensions where populism challenges liberal norms. Like religious dogmas, ideologies can blind us to shared needs, making compromise feel like betrayal. Only reason can soften these lines, as later examples show.

3. Political leaders manipulate fear of the "Other" to rally support

Fear is politics' oldest currency. By conjuring an "other," a foreign threat or a domestic scapegoat, leaders unify followers, deflecting blame from their own failures. This mirrors the in-group/out-group dynamics of earlier chapters but with a twist: politics weaponizes fear with precision. Ancient Rome's senators vilified Carthage to justify wars; modern campaigns demonize immigrants or rivals to win votes. The "other" becomes a shadow, vague enough to project any sin, real or imagined.

History brims with examples. In apartheid South Africa, the National Party stoked White fear of Black "swart gevaar" (Black danger) to maintain segregationist rule. In the U.S., McCarthyism's Red Scare from the 1940s to the 1950s painted communists as lurking traitors, ruining lives to bolster political careers. Today, fear persists. Brexit's 2016 campaign leaned on anti-migrant rhetoric, framing the EU as an alien threat. These tactics work because fear bypasses reason, tapping primal instincts. But they sustain conflict and deepen divisions at the very moments when dialogue could build bridges. This is the cycle that this book aims to challenge and transform.

- **Historical Examples with Detail**

1. The Cold War (1947–1991)

The Cold War was not fought with armies clashing on open fields but with ideas, such as capitalism versus communism, that divided the globe. After World War II, the United States and the Soviet Union emerged as superpowers, each preaching a vision: America's free markets and democracy against the USSR's classless state. This ideological rift split nations such as East and West Germany, and North and South Korea, and fueled proxy wars. Vietnam, from 1955 to 1975, saw three million die as the U.S.-backed South battled the communist North. The Soviet invasion of Afghanistan from 1979 to 1989 killed two million, with U.S.-funded mujahideen sowing chaos that eventually birthed al-Qaeda.

The stakes were apocalyptic. The 1962 Cuban Missile Crisis brought humanity closest to nuclear war, with U.S. and Soviet brinkmanship risking billions of lives. Fear drove the divide: propaganda painted the "other" as existential evil. Soviet posters showed capitalist wolves, while U.S. films cast Reds as spies. Yet moments of reason, like the détente of the 1980s or Gorbachev's reforms, eased tensions, proving politics could pivot. The Cold War shows ideology's power to fracture, but also humanity's capacity to pull back when reason prevails.

2. The French Revolution (1789–1799)

The French Revolution began with noble ideals: liberty, equality, fraternity, challenging a monarchy that starved its people while nobles feasted. But ideology turned volatile. The 1789 storming of the Bastille sparked hope, but factions such as the Girondins and Jacobins clashed over how to remake France. The Reign of Terror from 1793 to 1794, led by Robespierre, saw guillotines claim 40,000 lives, from royals to peasants, as "enemies of the revolution" were purged. Fear of counter-revolution fueled paranoia, turning ideals into dogma.

Externally, revolutionary France waged wars against monarchist Europe, spreading republicanism but also chaos. By 1799, Napoleon's rise swapped one autocracy for another, showing ideology's fragility when unchecked. The legacy of the revolution, rooted in democratic ideals yet marred by violent excess, exposes the dual nature of politics: a powerful engine for progress that turns destructive when passion overtakes reason. This duality mirrors the religious rigidity explored in Chapter 2, reinforcing the need for a rational and balanced approach.

3. The Nigerian civil war (1967–1970)

Nigeria's civil war, also called the Biafran War, was a post-colonial tragedy rooted in politics and region. After independence from Britain in 1960, Nigeria's diverse ethnic groups, including the Hausa Fulani, Yoruba, and Igbo, vied for power in a fragile federation. Political coups in 1966, seen as Igbo led, sparked anti-Igbo pogroms in the north, killing thousands. The Igbo dominated southeast seceded as Biafra in 1967, seeking self-rule. The federal government, backed by Britain and the USSR, fought to preserve unity.

The war was brutal: 1 to 3 million died, mostly from starvation as Nigeria blockaded Biafra. Political ambition, such as control of oil rich regions, and ethnic mistrust drove the conflict, with leaders like Gowon and Ojukwu rallying followers through fear of "the other." Biafra's surrender in 1970 ended the war, but scars linger in Nigeria's ethnic politics. Reconciliation efforts, like federal power sharing, show politics' potential to mend, aligning with your unity vision.

- **Outlined Viewpoint**

1. Propaganda amplifies political division

Propaganda turns political divides into chasms, shaping minds with calculated narratives. Nazi Germany mastered this. Goebbels' films like *Triumph of the Will* glorified Hitler, while posters vilified Jews as subhuman, paving the way for the Holocaust's six million deaths. Radio, newspapers, and rallies made hate feel patriotic. Similarly, Stalin's USSR used Pravda to paint capitalists as parasites, justifying purges that killed millions.

Today, propaganda evolves as social media amplifies it. Russia's 2014 Crimea annexation leaned on TV disinformation, framing Ukraine as fascist. In the United States, partisan outlets fuel polarization, with 2020 election misinformation sparking Capitol riots. Propaganda works by drowning reason, making others monstrous. Countering it requires critical thinking, media literacy, and rigorous fact-checking, the essential pillars of a reasoned and unified discourse.

2. Modern populism and polarization as historical patterns

Today's political divides echo history's. Populism, seen in slogans like Trump's 'Make America Great Again' or Bolsonaro's anti-elite crusades, revives fear-driven politics through appeals to cultural identity and tradition. It casts elites, immigrants, or minorities as "others," much like McCarthy's communists or apartheid's Black population. Polarization splits societies. Pew Research shows 80 percent of Americans view the other party as a "threat to the nation's well-being" (2020).

In Europe, Brexit and far-right surges fracture unity.

These mirror past ideological battles, including the French Revolution's factions and the Cold War's camps, where dogma trumped dialogue. Social media, like propaganda, accelerates this, creating echo chambers. Yet history suggests hope. Post World War I reconciliation birthed the League of Nations, flawed but forward thinking. Today's polarization, while fierce, can yield to reason if we prioritize shared goals such as climate and health over tribal wins.

3. Moments of political compromise show unity's possibilities

Politics can heal when reason guides it. South Africa's post-apartheid transition from 1990 to 1994 is a beacon. After decades of racial segregation, Nelson Mandela and F.W. de Klerk negotiated an end to apartheid, averting civil war. The 1993 interim constitution and 1994 elections, though tense, gave all South Africans a voice. The Truth and Reconciliation Commission faced past horrors, choosing justice over vengeance.

Elsewhere, Colombia's 2016 peace deal with FARC rebels ended a 50-year conflict, reintegrating fighters despite public anger. Even the Cold War's end saw compromise, as Reagan and Gorbachev's 1987 INF Treaty cut nuclear arsenals, easing global fear. These moments show politics bending toward unity when leaders value humanity over power. They foreshadow the vision in Chapter 6, proving division is not fate.

Divided We Stand

CHAPTER 5

THE COST OF CONFLICT: WHAT WE LOSE

Overview

Conflict, whether sparked by religious zeal, regional pride, or political ambition, exacts a price no victor can repay. The swords of crusades, the bombs of revolutions, the machetes of ethnic purges all leave behind a ledger of loss that stretches beyond battlefields. Lives are extinguished, families shattered, and communities uprooted. Ancient temples crumble, libraries burn, and landscapes scar under the weight of war. Economies falter, trust erodes, and the collective energy needed to tackle humanity's greatest challenges such as climate change, pandemics, and inequality is squandered in cycles of division.

This chapter tallies the toll of conflicts driven by the forces dissected in earlier chapters: religion's dogmas (Chapter 2), region's borders (Chapter 3), and politics' ideologies (Chapter 4), all rooted in the tribal instincts of our biology (Chapter 1). World War II's millions dead, Syria's displaced masses, and Palmyra's shattered ruins are not isolated tragedies but symptoms of a deeper failure to choose reason over rivalry. Beyond numbers such as casualties, refugees, and dollars, conflict steals our shared heritage, scars psyches across generations, and stalls progress on existential threats. By quantifying these costs, this chapter underscores the urgency of breaking the cycle. Division isn't just destructive; it's a betrayal of our potential to thrive as one species on one planet. Here, we mourn what's lost and ignite the resolve to forge alternatives.

- **Core Insights with Depth**

1. Wars destroy lives, economies, and heritage

The most visible cost of conflict is its body count: men, women, children reduced to statistics in history's grim accounting. But the ripple effects are vast. Wars orphan generations, bankrupt nations, and erase treasures that anchor our collective story. A single bullet ends a life; a campaign can end a culture. The economic drain is staggering: rebuilding cities, treating wounded, or resettling refugees diverts wealth from education, healthcare, or innovation. The World Bank estimates global conflicts cost $14 trillion annually in direct and indirect losses, enough to end extreme poverty several times over.

Heritage, too, is a casualty. When temples, churches, mosques, or libraries fall, we lose threads to our past, artifacts that remind us of shared humanity. In the misty silence of Kashmir's mountains lie the broken bones of temples, once vibrant with chants, bells, and light. These were not just structures of stone, but sanctuaries of thought, of devotion, of a people's soul. Over centuries, they were defaced, abandoned, and forgotten, not by time but by design. The valley, once a beacon of Shaivism, now carries the sorrow of erased memory. The destruction of the Bamiyan Buddhas in 2001 was not the first wound to our shared heritage; it was one more echo in a long dirge. For when conflict chooses conquest over culture, it does more than raze monuments; it steals futures, silences identities, and buries the very heartbeat of civilization. This loss, tying back to religion's fervour (Chapter 2) and region's claims (Chapter 3), demands we question why we let division rob us so thoroughly.

2. Division fosters mistrust, hindering global challenges

Conflict doesn't just kill; it poisons trust, the glue of cooperation. When religious, regional, or political divides harden, neighbours become strangers, and nations turn inward. This mistrust cripples our ability to face shared threats. Climate change, with its rising seas and deadly heatwaves, requires global action; yet, the 2015 Paris Agreement's goals lag as countries bicker over emissions cuts. The IPCC warns a 3°C warming looms by 2100 without unity, risking 20% of global GDP and billions displaced. Pandemics, too, expose division's cost: during COVID-19, vaccine hoarding by rich nations left poorer ones vulnerable, prolonging the crisis.

Mistrust's roots are historical. After the Crusades, Christian-Muslim suspicion lingered, hampering cooperation. Cold

War rivalries delayed smallpox eradication until détente allowed WHO campaigns to succeed. Today, geopolitical spats such as U.S. and China trade wars and Russia and West sanctions stall climate talks or AI governance. Like wolves snarling over territory (Chapter 1), we prioritize "us" over "all," forgetting that a burning planet or runaway virus spares no one. This point heightens the urgency behind the narrative: division isn't just tragic; it's suicidal.

3. Conflict distracts from humanity's potential to innovate and thrive

Every missile launched, every border fortified, is a choice to divert human ingenuity from creation to destruction. Conflict consumes resources such as time, minds, and money that could solve hunger, cure diseases, or explore the stars. The U.S. spent $8 trillion on post 9/11 wars, per Brown University, enough to fund global clean energy for a decade. Imagine engineers designing tanks instead of crafting solar grids, or scientists building bombs rather than vaccines. Conflict doesn't just kill; it starves our future.

This distraction betrays our potential. The Renaissance, born in relative peace, gave us Michelangelo and Galileo; the internet, a Cold War byproduct, flourished in collaboration. When we fight over Gods, lands, or ideologies, we lose focus on what makes us human: our capacity to dream and build together. The Syrian war's brain drain, with doctors and teachers fleeing, robs not just Syria but the world of talent. Connecting to the political dynamics discussed in Chapter 4, this shows how power games squander collective genius and reinforces the plea for a rational pivot to unity.

- **Historical Examples with Detail**

1. World War II (1939–1945)

World War II was humanity's deadliest conflict, a maelstrom of ideology and territory fueled by fascism's rise and regional ambitions. Nazi Germany's quest for Lebensraum and Japan's imperial dreams clashed with Allied resistance, costing between 70 and 85 million lives, or about 3% of the global population. The Holocaust alone murdered 6 million Jews, along with millions of Romani, disabled individuals, and others, erasing communities and their contributions. Atomic bombs on Hiroshima and Nagasaki killed 200,000 people, leaving survivors with physical and mental scars.

The economic toll was vast: Europe and Asia's cities, such as Dresden and Tokyo, lay in rubble, with rebuilding costs reaching trillions in adjusted dollars. Cultural losses stung deeply as Poland's libraries burned and China's artifacts were looted. The war's mistrust fueled the Cold War, delaying global cooperation. Yet its end birthed the United Nations, a flawed but hopeful step toward unity, hinting at reason's potential. World War II's scale reveals conflict's waste of lives, wealth, and heritage, making the search for alternatives all the more urgent.

2. The Syrian civil war (2011–Present)

Sparked by Arab Spring protests against Assad's regime, Syria's civil war blends politics and sectarian divides. What began as demands for reform spiralled into a proxy battle, with Russia and Iran backing Assad, and the U.S. and Turkey aiding rebels. Over 500,000 have died, according to UN estimates, with 6.8 million internally displaced and 5.5 million refugees flooding Turkey, Jordan, and Europe. Cities like Aleppo, once vibrant, are now rubble; schools and hospitals lie ruined.

The economic cost exceeds $1 trillion, according to the World Bank, crippling Syria's future. Refugees strain host nations, with Lebanon holding 1.5 million, one-fifth of its population, fueling tensions. Culturally, Syria's heritage, including the Umayyad Mosque and Krak des Chevaliers, suffers looting or bombardment. The war's global ripple, from Europe's 2015 migrant crisis to jihadist networks, shows division's reach. Grassroots aid, such as the Syrian diaspora rebuilding schools, offers glimmers of hope, aligning with our unity vision, but the toll screams for change.

3. The destruction of Palmyra (2015)

In 2015, ISIS dynamited Palmyra, a 2,000-year-old Syrian city and UNESCO World Heritage Site, erasing Roman temples, arches, and tombs. This was not collateral damage but deliberate; ISIS targeted "idolatrous" relics to assert ideological purity, echoing religion's rigidity (Chapter 2). Palmyra, a crossroads of Greek, Persian, and Roman cultures, symbolized shared humanity. Its loss, with columns toppled and artifacts smashed, robs us of history's lessons.

The destruction cost millions to partially restore, diverting funds from Syria's starving population. It also fueled propaganda, as ISIS videos spread fear and deepened global divides. Yet international efforts, such as UNESCO's 3D modeling to preserve Palmyra's memory, show the spark of cooperation. This case, tied to Syria's broader war, illustrates conflict's assault on heritage and urges rational stewardship over destruction.

- **Outlined Viewpoint**

1. Data proving the toll in concrete terms

Numbers ground the abstract. World War II's 70 to 85 million deaths included 50 million civilians, according to historian estimates, with $4 trillion (in 1945 dollars) in damages. Syria's war displaced 13 million, half its population, costing $1.2 trillion by 2020, according to UN reports. Globally, 100 million people are displaced today, according to UNHCR, with conflicts draining $14 trillion yearly, according to the Institute for Economics and Peace. Cultural losses are harder to quantify: 24% of UNESCO World Heritage Sites face conflict threats, from Mali's Timbuktu to Yemen's Sana'a. These figures, whether in lives, dollars, or heritage, make the price of division undeniable and reinforce our collective call for unity.

2. Psychological impacts like intergenerational trauma

Conflict's wounds linger in minds. Intergenerational trauma, pain passed through families, shapes societies long after guns fall silent. Holocaust survivors' children often carry anxiety or guilt, studies show, with epigenetic changes linked to stress. In Rwanda, genocide orphans face stigma, while perpetrators' descendants grapple with shame, according to Reconciliation Rwanda reports. Syria's refugees report PTSD at rates above 30%, according to WHO, with youth losing education and hope.

This trauma fuels cycles. Mistrust from past wars, such as Japan-Korea tensions over the 1910 to 1945 occupation, stokes new clashes. Like mistrust's global impact (Core insight with depth 2), it hinders healing. Yet therapy programs, such as Israel's trauma centers for Gaza conflict victims, show reason's role in breaking cycles, aligning with our call for empathy and unity.

3. Connection to current global issues

Division stalls solutions to existential threats. Climate change demands unity, yet COP28 (2023) saw oil-rich nations resist fossil fuel phase-outs, echoing Cold War era mistrust. The IPCC projects 250 million climate refugees by 2050 if action lags. Pandemics expose similar flaws: COVAX aimed for global vaccine equity, but rich nations hoarded doses, delaying recovery. WHO estimates 7 million excess COVID deaths by 2023. AI governance, another frontier, falters as U.S.-China rivalry blocks global standards, risking unchecked systems.

These challenges tie to Chapters 2 to 4: religious divides, such as climate denialism in the evangelical U.S.; regional pride, such as India-China border spats over shared rivers; and politics, such as populist anti-science rhetoric. Conflict's distraction, as highlighted in 'Core insight with depth'- 3, wastes time we do not have, making our rational unity argument not just a moral necessity but a survival imperative.

CHAPTER 6

THE PATH TO UNITY:
REASON AS OUR GUIDE

Overview

The scars of conflict, etched in graves, ruins, and mistrust, tell a story of division, but they also whisper of possibility. Humanity, for all its flaws, is not condemned to repeat the cycles of religion's dogmas (Chapter 2), region's borders (Chapter 3), or politics' power games (Chapter 4). Rooted in the tribal instincts of our biology (Chapter 1) yet gifted with reason, we can choose a different path. Chapter 5 laid bare the staggering cost of conflict: lives lost, heritage erased, progress stalled, making the case undeniable that unity is not just desirable but essential for our survival.

This chapter proposes a vision for overcoming division by embracing three pillars: reason, empathy, and shared goals. Reason lets us question narratives that pit "us" against "them," revealing our common humanity beneath the masks of faith, place, or ideology. Empathy, the act of seeing through another's eyes, builds bridges where walls once stood. And shared goals, born of global challenges like climate change, pandemics, or AI's risks, demand cooperation, turning unity from an ideal into a practical necessity. Historical triumphs, from the Peace of Westphalia to the Montreal Protocol and South Africa's Truth and Reconciliation Commission, prove we have walked this path before. By investing in education, harnessing technology, and taking concrete steps such as interfaith dialogues, cross-border partnerships, and global reforms, we can forge a future where division yields to connection. This is not utopia; it is a choice, guided by the reason that makes us human.

- **Core Insights with Depth**

1. Reason allows us to question divisive narratives and recognize our common humanity

Reason is our sharpest tool, the gift that sets us apart from wolves snarling over territory or birds fighting for scraps (Chapter 1). It lets us step back, interrogate the stories we are told, about Gods, nations, or enemies, and see them for what they are: human constructs, not eternal truths. The narrative of "us vs. them," whether preached from pulpits (Chapter 2), etched in borders (Chapter 3), or shouted in campaigns (Chapter 4), thrives on unchallenged assumptions. Reason dismantles them, asking: Why fear the stranger? What makes my flag worth more than yours?

This questioning reveals our shared humanity. Our DNA is 99.9% identical; our needs for food, love, and safety are universal. A mother in Gaza weeps for her lost child just as one in Tel Aviv does; a Hindu farmer in rural India dreams of rain and a good harvest, just like a Christian farmer in Argentina or a Muslim one in Sudan. Reason strips away the labels, Jew, Arab, Hindu, Muslim, Christian, atheist, that divide us, revealing that we are one species sharing a fragile, wounded planet. Philosophers like David Hume, as mentioned earlier, warned that factions and fanaticism arise when passion trumps reflection. Reason, in contrast, bridges the divide between mosque and temple, synagogue and church, by anchoring us in shared truths rather than inherited dogmas. The historical examples below show reason not as a passive ideal but as an active force that has reshaped conflicts and offers a blueprint for peace in our fractured world.

2. Empathy, grounded in understanding others' perspectives, can bridge divides

If reason clears the mind, empathy opens the heart. To empathize is to inhabit another's world, to feel the weight of a refugee's loss, the sting of a minority's exclusion, or the fear behind a rival's defiance. Unlike sympathy, which pities from afar, empathy demands effort: listening to stories, acknowledging pain, even when it challenges our own. It is the antidote to the in-group out-group traps of religion, region, and politics, turning "others" into kin.

Empathy does not erase differences, it honors them. A Jew and a Palestinian sharing grief over lost homes, as in grassroots groups like Parents Circle (Chapter 3), find common ground without denying their truths. This bridge-building is vital because division thrives on ignorance. Crusaders and Saracens

(Chapter 2) fought partly because they rarely met as equals. Empathy, paired with reason, fosters dialogue where dogma once ruled. South Africa's reconciliation, detailed below, shows empathy's power to heal even the deepest wounds, a model for transcending today's divides.

3. Global challenges require cooperation, making unity a practical necessity

Unity is not a luxury, it is a survival strategy. Climate change, with its floods and fires, does not respect borders; the IPCC (Intergovernmental Panel on Climate Change) projects 1 billion climate migrants by 2050 if we fail to act. Pandemics, like COVID-19's 7 million deaths, exploit division. Vaccine inequity cost lives when nations hoarded doses. AI, advancing faster than laws, risks chaos without global rules. A 2023 study warned of "catastrophic" misuse if governance lags. These threats, unlike past wars, do not pick sides, they imperil all.

Cooperation is the only path. The Montreal Protocol's success, explored below, proves nations can unite when stakes are clear. Smaller challenges too, like water scarcity and cybercrime, demand shared solutions. Politics may rally voters by demonizing foreigners, but survival rallies humans by demanding we work as one. Unity, rooted in reason and empathy, becomes practical, not a feel-good slogan but a necessity as urgent as air. This ties to Chapter 5's losses: if conflict wastes our potential, cooperation harnesses it.

- **Historical Examples with Detail**

1. The peace of Westphalia (1648)

The Thirty Years' War ravaged Europe, killing 8 million as Catholics and Protestants fought over faith and power. By 1648, exhaustion forced a reckoning. Diplomats from across the continent met in Westphalia, negotiating for months to end the bloodshed. The resulting treaties established principles of sovereignty, where nations could choose their religion, and coexistence, curbing holy wars. It was not perfect: borders stayed contentious (Chapter 3), and power struggles persisted (Chapter 4). But it marked a triumph of reason over dogma.

Westphalia's legacy endures in modern diplomacy, with UN charters balancing state rights with global goals. It showed that even bitter foes, steeped in religious and political divides, could prioritize survival through dialogue. A beacon, reason can tame conflict's chaos, guiding us toward unity when passion cools and minds engage.

2. The Montreal protocol (1987)

In the 1980s, scientists sounded an alarm: chlorofluorocarbons (CFCs), used in aerosols and fridges, were tearing a hole in the ozone layer, risking skin cancer and ecosystem collapse. Unlike today's climate debates, nations acted swiftly. The 1987 Montreal Protocol, signed by 197 countries, banned CFCs, with rich nations funding poorer ones' transitions. By 2020, the ozone hole was shrinking, per NASA, a rare environmental win.

This success hinged on reason, where science trumped skepticism, and shared goals, as no nation wanted a UV-scorched planet. It overcame political divides (Chapter 4), with Reagan's U.S.

and Thatcher's UK leading despite industry pushback. This stands as evidence that when we prioritize facts and cooperation, humanity can unite against global threats and offers a powerful model for confronting today's challenges like climate change and AI risks.

3. The truth and reconciliation commission (South Africa, 1996–2003)

After apartheid's fall in 1994, South Africa faced a fractured future. Decades of racial oppression, with Black townships razed and activists jailed, left 21,000 dead and millions wounded. Civil war loomed. Instead, Nelson Mandela and Desmond Tutu launched the Truth and Reconciliation Commission (TRC). From 1996 to 2003, it heard 22,000 testimonies, victims sharing pain and perpetrators confessing crimes, in public hearings blending reason and empathy.

The TRC did not erase scars; some criticized its amnesty for torturers. But it averted vengeance, forging a shared narrative. Blacks and Whites wept together, seeing each other's humanity. By 2003, it had granted 1,200 amnesties and recommended reparations, rebuilding trust. This stands as a masterclass in unity, where reason structured the process, empathy bridged the divides, and a shared goal of peace guided both. It ties to all chapters, offering a powerful example of how humanity can rise above the barriers of religion, region, and politics.

- **Outlined Viewpoint**

1. Education's role in fostering critical thinking to combat dogma

Education is reason's forge. By teaching critical thinking, how to question, analyze, not parrot, schools can dismantle divisive narratives. Finland's curriculum, emphasizing media literacy, cuts through propaganda, with students ranking tops in discerning fake news (PISA 2018). In Rwanda, post-genocide education bans ethnic labels, fostering a unified identity. Contrast this with dogmatic systems: Taliban schools in Afghanistan teach rigid faith, perpetuating conflict.

Globally, education's reach matters. UNESCO notes 60% of youth lack basic literacy in conflict zones, trapping them in cycles of fear. Investing here, $340 billion annually per UN estimates, could break dogma's grip, teaching kids to see shared humanity over tribal lines. Education is essential; it lays the foundation for questioning the absolutes of religion, the divisions of region, and the deceptions of politics, paving the way toward unity.

2. Technology as a tool for connection

Technology, wielded well, shrinks divides. The internet, born from Cold War collaboration, connects 5 billion people, per 2023 data. Social media, despite fueling polarization, also unites. #BlackLivesMatter sparked global solidarity, linking U.S. protests to Nigeria's #EndSARS. Platforms like Zoom enabled 2020's virtual climate summits, bypassing borders. Even AI, a risk without governance, can bridge gaps; translation apps break language barriers, aiding refugees.

History supports this: the telegraph sped 19th-century peace talks, much as satellites now track climate data for shared solutions. But technology's dual edge, such as misinformation and surveillance, demands reason to steer it. The potential of technology as a unifying force deserves to be championed, encouraging the creation of cross-border platforms such as open-source science hubs that foster empathy and shared goals, while breaking down the barriers built by religion and politics.

3. Practical steps: Interfaith initiatives, Cross-Border collaborations, Global Governance Reforms

Unity requires action, not just ideals. 'Interfaith initiatives', like the Parliament of the World's Religions, unite 10,000+ annually to tackle poverty or peace, countering religious strife. Local efforts, such as Jordan's 2004 Amman Message or India's interfaith NGOs, build trust block by block. 'Cross-border collaborations' work too: the EU's Erasmus program swaps 1 million students yearly, blending regional identities. The Nile Basin Initiative, despite Egypt and Ethiopia tensions, shares water data, easing conflict.

'Global governance reforms' are toughest but vital. The UN, born after WWII, needs teeth; veto reforms, according to 2023 proposals, could curb Security Council gridlock. A global AI treaty modelled on Montreal could align nations before risks spiral. These steps, grounded in reason, scale empathy: interfaith talks humanize "others," cross-border projects share stakes, and reforms align incentives. These examples show that unity is not something we can merely hope for; it must be deliberately built through effort and action.

CHAPTER 7

A CALL TO ACTION:
WHY UNITY MATTERS NOW

Overview

We are animals, social yes, but animals still, driven by instincts that spark conflict over Gods, borders, and power. Yet, one trait sets us apart: our rationality, the spark that can ignite peace or fuel destruction. History's ledger, from crusades to genocides and revolutions, shows conflict's toll: lives lost, heritage erased, trust broken. What's done cannot be undone, but we can choose differently. Chapter 6 charted a path through reason, empathy, and shared goals, with Westphalia, Montreal, and South Africa proving unity's power. Now, we face a choice: cling to hate, perpetuating division, or embrace reason, forging harmony.

This chapter is a fervent call to act, declaring unity urgent for survival. Climate crises flood our homes, AI risks outpace laws, social fractures turn neighbours into foes, and division wastes the resources we need to fight these threats. We are one species, sons and daughters of the same divine under countless names, born and departing this planet the same way. Conflict solves nothing; history proves it breeds only ruin. Together, we can achieve peace and prosperity, a harmony that heals our world. The Paris Agreement and COVAX show unity's spark; reason, as 18th-century philosopher David Hume urged, can douse factionalism. Unity is not a dream; it is a daily choice to say no to hate. The stakes, our planet and our future, are monumental. Will we choose destruction, or a world where reason wins?

- **Core Insights with Depth**

1. Conflict wastes resources we need to solve existential threats

Like wolves guarding their pack (Chapter 1), we humans fight, over faiths (Chapter 2), lands (Chapter 3), ideologies (Chapter 4), but at what cost? Every war, every wall drains what we need to face existential crises. Climate change scorches our planet, with 2024's record heat, per NASA, displacing 20 million with floods, according to UNHCR. Without unity, the IPCC's projected $54 trillion in damages by 2050 will bankrupt us. AI's unchecked growth risks chaos, as 2023 talks faltered over U.S. and China rivalry, per UN reports. Social divides, like U.S. polarization costing $1 trillion yearly in lost trust (Pew Research), sap our strength.

History screams: conflict breeds destruction, not solutions. The Crusades left mistrust (Chapter 2), Rwanda's genocide orphaned a nation (Chapter 3), the Cold War risked annihilation (Chapter 4). We are animals, yes, but our rationality can redirect this energy, turning engineers to green tech, leaders to AI treaties, and citizens to dialogue. Chapter 5's $14 trillion annual conflict toll could end poverty; reason lets us choose prosperity over ruin. Hate solves nothing; unity saves everything.

2. Our shared biology and planet demand a collective response

We are one species, our 99.9% identical DNA coding the same hopes and fears, a laugh in Mumbai mirrors one in Mexico City. We share one planet, its air and water sustaining us all. Yet, as David Hume warned, we form factions, religious, regional, political, driven by instinct over reason, fueling "violent animosities."

Beneath these labels, we are sons and daughters of one divine, called God, Allah, Brahman, or countless names, born and leaving this earth the same: fragile, human, equal.

This unity demands collective action. A virus in one city becomes a global plague; a factory's smoke warms every shore. Chapter 5 showed how division delayed progress, vaccine hoarding prolonged COVID, mistrust slowed climate talks. We come from different races, places, and paths, but our fates intertwine. Reason, Hume's antidote, sees past factions to our shared essence. Chapter 6's triumphs, Montreal's ozone fix and South Africa's healing, prove we can act as one. Hate divides; rationality unites, creating a harmony that transcends our differences.

3. Unity Is not utopian; It's a practical choice we can make daily

We are social animals, prone to tribalism, but our thinking sets us apart. Rationality can work wonders, building bridges where hate builds walls, or wreak havoc when ignored, as history's ruins show (Chapter 5). Conflict never solved anything; it only destroyed, think of WWII's 80 million dead or Syria's shattered cities. We cannot undo the past, but we can say no to hate by choosing unity daily. It is not utopia, it is a neighbour listening across a political divide, a teacher challenging stereotypes, a voter backing peace.

This choice is practical. Chapter 6's heroes, diplomats at Westphalia, scientists at Montreal, made it, as did Mandela's reconcilers. Small acts compound: a 2023 study found community projects cut prejudice by 30%

through contact. We are all human, on different paths but sharing one journey. Together, we can forge peace and prosperity, a harmony where diverse voices, every faith and every creed, sing as one. Reason makes it real; the choice is ours, destruction or a thriving world.

- **Modern examples with detail**

1. The Paris Agreement (2015)

In 2015, 196 nations met in Paris, not as foes but as stewards of one planet, to fight climate change, a threat that spares no race or creed. The Paris Agreement pledged to cap warming at 1.5 to 2°C, uniting rich and poor, East and West, under science's clarity. Flaws persist, as 2023's COP28 lagged on fossil fuel cuts, but it has driven one trillion dollars in clean energy investment since 2015, according to UN data, with solar costs down 80%. Grassroots voices, including Pacific Island activists, pushed leaders, showing that every human counts.

Paris echoes Chapter 6's Montreal Protocol: reason, driven by data, and shared survival triumphed over division. It proves we can choose unity over hate, even amid politics (Chapter 4) or borders (Chapter 3). It offers a spark, an invitation to join climate marches, support green policies, and take small steps as one species sharing one earth, building harmony through collective action.

2. Global vaccine efforts (2020–Present)

COVID-19's seven million deaths (Chapter 5) showed division's cost as nations hoarded and borders closed. Yet, COVAX, launched by WHO and GAVI in 2020, sought to share 2 billion vaccine doses equitably, prioritizing the vulnerable regardless of faith or flag. It stumbled because rich nations took 70% of early shots, per Oxfam, but reached 1 billion doses across 144 countries by 2023, saving countless lives. Scientists shared formulas, and companies like

AstraZeneca licensed vaccines, a nod to our shared humanity.

COVAX ties to Chapter 2's interfaith aid and Chapter 3's EU. Collective action, though imperfect, works when reason guides. It is a call to reject hate's silos and choose solidarity, support global health, and advocate equity. As one people under one God, our choices shape a world where no one is left behind, a step toward peace.

- **Outlined Viewpoint**

1. Reflect on personal biases

Unity begins within. Our animal instincts, tribal and territorial (Chapter 1), fuel biases: a person from Religious Group A eyeing someone from Group B warily (Chapter 2), a Parisian dismissing a villager (Chapter 3), a liberal scorning a conservative (Chapter 4). Reason, our human edge, demands we question: Why do I judge by creed, accent, or politics? Harvard's Implicit Bias Test shows 80% of us harbour prejudices (2023 data). Try it, or read a rival's story, a Sikh's memoir, or a Trump voter's blog. This mirrors Chapter 6's empathy: seeing others as fellow humans, not "others," dismantles hate. It is not shame, it is strength, a daily choice for harmony.

2. Small actions

Peace isn't built in grand strokes alone. Engage with "others": join a diverse club (Chapter 2), volunteer across town (Chapter 3), or debate kindly online (Chapter 4). Support inclusive policies: back leaders who unite like New Zealand's Ardern post-2019 mosque attacks or local laws for equity like Canada's 2023 diversity rules. Learn shared challenges: read IPCC (Intergovernmental Panel on Climate Change) reports, join AI ethics talks, or march for climate: knowledge fuels collective will, per Chapter 6's education.

History's lessons Truth and Reconciliation Commission's (TRC's) testimonies (Chapter 6), Paris's pledges started small. A 2023 study shows community projects gardens, refugee aid cut bias 30% by fostering contact. As one species, our acts ripple: a conversation sparks peace, a vote builds prosperity. Choose reason, reject hate, and harmony grows.

3. A hopeful vision

Picture a world where reason triumphs over our animal instincts. Schools teach thinking, not dogma, dissolving faith's walls (Chapter 2) and borders' lines (Chapter 3). Tech unites, global forums tame AI, as the internet linked scientists (Chapter 6). Nations share: vaccines reach all, climate funds lift the poorest, unlike Chapter 5's losses. Conflicts fade, no crusades, no genocides, because we see one humanity, sons and daughters of one divine, on one planet.

This is no fantasy. Paris's pact, COVAX's doses, South Africa's peace show it's real. By 2050, 10 billion could thrive, clean energy lights cities, AI heals, communities blend as equals. Together, we achieve peace and prosperity, a harmony where every path shines. History proves conflict destroys; reason proves unity builds. The choice is ours: hate's ruin or a world where we stand as one.

AFTERWORD

As I pen these final words, I imagine you, dear readers around the globe, turning the pages of this book: from the primal instincts that first divided us to the wars, borders, and ideologies that kept us apart, and finally to the fragile yet fierce hope of unity. Writing this book has been like holding a lantern to humanity's story, illuminating both its shadows and its light. We are, as I have come to see, a species of contradictions: animals wired for tribes yet gifted with reason, builders of walls yet dreamers of bridges.

Through these chapters, we have walked battlefields stained by faith, traced borders drawn by pride, and unravelled the power games of politics. We have mourned the losses of lives, heritage, and trust torn away by conflict. But we have also glimpsed what is possible: treaties forged in reason, science uniting nations, communities healing through empathy. The truth has crystallized for me, and I hope for you as well: division is not our destiny. We are sons and daughters of one earth, one divine by countless names, bound by the same heartbeat and the same fleeting time on this planet.

This book began with a question that haunted me: Why do we fracture our shared home? The answer lies not in Gods, maps, or manifestos, but in choices we make when we let fear outshout reason, when we forget our shared breath. History whispers a warning that conflict breeds only ruin. But it also sings of hope: from Westphalia's peace to Paris's pact, from South Africa's truth to COVAX's reach, we have proven we can choose differently. Reason, our brightest gift, lights the path to peace, prosperity, and harmony.

Now, the lantern passes to you. This is not the end but a beginning. In your hands lies the power to question biases, those quiet prejudices about faith, place, or politics that linger in us all. In your voice rests the chance to speak across divides, to listen where others shout. In your choices, whether as small as a kind word or as bold as a vote for unity, lie the seeds of a world where we stand as one. The stakes are vast: a planet warming, technologies racing ahead, fractures widening. But so is our potential, if we dare to think, to feel, and to act.

I dream of a day when children of every creed play under the same sky, unshadowed by hate; when we solve crises not as tribes but as kin; when our differences become not walls but colors woven together in unity. This dream lives in you: in every step you take to say no to division and yes to reason. Together, we can weave harmony from discord, a legacy for those yet to come. So go gently, think deeply, and choose bravely. The world awaits our unity, and the time is now.

अयं निजः परो वेति गणना लघुचेतसाम् ।
उदारचरितानां तु वसुधैव कुटुम्बकम् ।।

"This is mine, that is yours - say the small-minded;
For those of noble character, the entire earth is one family."

Mahopanishad (Chapter 6, Verse 72)